GR

Step By Step Beginners Instruction To The Complete Growing Techniques & Troubleshooting Solutions

SHANE BOWIE

Copyright © 2024 By Shane Bowie

All Rights Reserved

Table of Contents

Introductory 5

CHAPTER ONE 8

   Advantages Of Pampas Grass Plantation 8

   Chaparral Grass Types 11

CHAPTER TWO 15

   Abiotic And Biotic Factors 15

   Levels Of Ph And Soil Preparation 19

CHAPTER THREE 23

   Choosing An Appropriate Site 23

   Establishing Pampas Grass 27

CHAPTER FOUR 32

   Pasture Maintenance 32

   Landscape Architecture With Grass Of The Pampas 36

CHAPTER FIVE 41

   Time Of Year Factors 41

   Methods For Propagation 46

CHAPTER SIX 52

   Troubleshooting And Common Problems .. 52

   Grass Harvesting On The Pampas 59

CHAPTER SEVEN 64
  Considerations And Impact On The Environment 64
  Summary 70
THE END 74

Introductory

The Pampas region, which encompasses portions of Argentina, Brazil, and Uruguay, is home to a variety of tall grasses that are collectively known as Pampas grass. In terms of cultivation, Cortaderia selloana is by far the most popular species.

Typically reaching heights of more than 10 feet (3 meters), the enormous, fluffy plumes of Pampas grass are a sight to behold. Species variation determines whether the plumes are white, pink, or silver in color.

Pampas grass is commonly utilized in gardens and landscaping for its beautiful and dramatic appearance, which is both functional and aesthetically pleasing. It should be mentioned that pampas grass may spread quickly and outcompete native flora, which makes it an invasive species in some areas outside of its natural environment. So, to keep it from wreaking havoc on the environment, its cultivation is limited.

Traditional South American communities have used pampas grass for a variety of purposes, including ornamentation and a number of artisan projects. Long, pointed leaves of this grass have long been a tool for weavers of baskets and other goods.

Even while pampas grass is beautiful, there are worries about the effects it will have on local ecosystems due to its invasiveness in some areas. So, it's crucial to know the rules and laws in your area about growing pampas grass before you plant it.

CHAPTER ONE
Advantages Of Pampas Grass Plantation

For those interested in landscaping or decorative gardening, pampas grass is a great plant to grow for a number of reasons. The following are a few possible benefits:

• The beautiful and decorative appearance of Pampas grass is one of its most valued qualities. Gardens and landscapes are adorned with the majestic and elegant huge plumes. The grass can be both a striking feature and a lovely background.

• The adaptability of Pampas grass makes it a great choice for a wide range of landscaping applications, from borders to privacy screens to as a stand-alone specimen plant. A sensation of seclusion and privacy can be achieved in outdoor areas by means of its lofty plumes.

• After it's established, pampas grass typically requires little care. In addition to thriving in a wide range of soil types, it is drought-tolerant. It can be kept in form and from growing too invasive with regular pruning.

• Soil Erosion Prevention: Pampas grass's vast root system is useful for this purpose. This makes it an excellent material to incorporate into landscape designs for slopes and other locations that are vulnerable to erosion.

- Wildlife Habitat: Insects and tiny birds can find shelter and food among the tall grasses of the Pampas. Animals may find refuge in the thick grass, which increases biodiversity in the area.

But before you start cultivating pampas grass, think about the problems and downsides that could arise. Its fast growth and potential to outcompete native plants make it an invasive species in some areas. It is critical to research local restrictions and implement measures to stop the spread of pampas grass before planting it.

Furthermore, pampas grass's dry foliage can be a fire threat in regions where wildfires are a concern. Planting and maintaining it appropriately, according to local guidelines and suggestions, is crucial.

Chaparral Grass Types

Pampas grass comes in a number of different types, each with its own set of quirks like size, coloration, and adaptability. Some common types are as follows:

- The pink-toned plumes of the Cortaderia selloana 'Rosea' species give the landscape a delicate, rosy tint. For a touch of variation from the standard white plumes, it's a popular option.

• The silvery-white plumes of the Cortaderia selloana 'Silver Comet' give it a subtler, more refined look. There is often a silvery gray hue to the foliage as well.

• 'Pumila' Cortaderia selloana is a dwarf pampas grass variant that thrives in tiny spaces, such as gardens or containers. It grows more compactly and produces shorter plumes.

• Andean Pampas Grass, or Cortaderia jubata, is a type of grass native to South America's Andes that resembles

Cortaderia selloana but is typically much bigger. It should be planted with care because it has become invasive in some areas.

• An additional visual element that adds visual interest to the plant is the golden band that runs around the edges of the leaves of the Cortaderia selloana 'Gold Band' variety.

It is important to think about things like garden size, desired grass height, and desired aesthetic while choosing a pampas grass variety. Also, keep in mind that different varieties of pampas grass have different growth patterns; some are more invasive than others. Before purchasing, consult with local officials or gardening professionals to find out if the variety is appropriate for your area and follows any rules against invasive species.

CHAPTER TWO
Abiotic And Biotic Factors

Although Pampas grass (Cortaderia spp.) may thrive in a variety of climates, how well it does in any one area is dependent on a number of factors. For the most part, pampas grass does well in the following climate and growing conditions:

• Pampas grass is most at home in regions with moderate to warm temperatures. In areas where the temperature doesn't consistently go below freezing for long periods of time, it does well (USDA hardiness zones 7–11).

- Pampas grass thrives in full sun, so be sure to give it at least 6-8 hours of sunshine daily so it may grow and bloom to its best potential.

- Pampas grass thrives in soil that drains properly. This plant is adaptable and may grow in a wide range of soil types, even sandy and loamy ones. Root rot is a real possibility in wet or heavy clay soils, thus it's best avoided.

- Although pampas grass may require frequent watering while it is just starting out, it is typically able to withstand periods of drought once it has reached maturity. After the plant has established itself, you can minimize the amount of water it needs to avoid overwatering.

• Prior to the start of new growth, pruning is typically done in the late winter or early spring. Destroying diseased or otherwise unhealthy foliage in this way encourages new development. The leaves of pampas grass are spiky, so handle them with care.

• To prevent overpopulation, make sure to leave enough space between plants of Pampas grass because it can grow to be fairly huge. This also aids in avoiding problems that could arise in areas where it is intrusive.

- It is important to research local rules and restrictions before growing pampas grass because the grass is invasive in some regions. The possibility that it would spread and displace native plants is why some areas have banned its growing.

For region-specific information before growing pampas grass, it's best to contact gardening professionals or agricultural extension agencies in your area. For pampas grass to thrive in your garden or landscape, it's important to choose a kind that's well-suited to your environment and available space.

Levels Of Ph And Soil Preparation

In order to grow pampas grass well, the soil must be prepared. The following are some recommendations for soil pH and preparation:

• Pampas grass can survive in a wide range of soil conditions, but it really comes into its own in areas with good drainage. Soils that are sandy or loamy tend to be better, but those that are very clay-rich should be avoided because they tend to become waterlogged.

• Pampas grass thrives on slightly acidic to neutral soils with pH values between 6.0 and 7.0. Go ahead and do a soil test to find out what your soil's pH is. Additions could be required if the pH falls below the ideal range.

• Before planting, amend the soil with compost or other organic material that has broken down. The soil's structure, drainage, and fertility are all enhanced as a result. To enhance drainage, you can incorporate perlite or coarse sand into soil that is typically heavy and has poor drainage properties.

• Create a hole that is wider than the pampas grass root ball by a minimum of two measures. To backfill the area around the plant, combine the excavated dirt with organic materials.

- Sow pampas grass seeds at the same depth as the seedlings were grown in the nursery. To keep root health in check, don't plant too deeply.

- To help the earth settle around the roots, water the newly planted pampas grass thoroughly. Overwatering can cause root rot in pampas grass, so be careful not to water too much during the establishment phase.

- Mulch the area surrounding the plant's base to keep soil moist, prevent weeds, and control the soil's temperature.

- Although pampas grass does not require extensive feeding, it can be fertilized in the spring using a balanced, slow-release fertilizer to encourage healthy development. Fertilize your plants sparingly to avoid stunted growth and unhealthy foliage.

It is recommended to modify these instructions according to your local weather and soil conditions because particular soil conditions can differ from one place to another. The long-term vitality and health of your pampas grass can be enhanced by keeping a close eye on it and making necessary adjustments to its watering and fertilizing routines.

CHAPTER THREE
Choosing An Appropriate Site

The success and longevity of pampas grass depend on your careful planting site selection. When deciding on the ideal spot, keep the following in mind:

• Pampas grass thrives in direct sunlight. Find a spot that gets at least six to eight hours of sunshine every day so it can grow and bloom to its full potential. Planting in partially shady places can lead to stunted development and fewer blossoms because of the lack of sunshine.

• Plumes of pampas grass can reach impressive heights when the grass grows to a considerable size. Make sure the plant will have enough room to grow to its full size. Overcrowding can be avoided and proper air circulation can be achieved with sufficient space between plants.

• The ideal soil for pampas grass is one that drains effectively. Because root rot can occur in wet circumstances, you should stay away from places with inadequate drainage. Think about adding organic matter or minerals like perlite or sand to the soil if it's heavy or doesn't drain well.

• Pay attention to areas where pampas grass could spread invasively. To make sure you're not breaking any rules regarding its cultivation, check local legislation and standards before planting.

• Although pampas grass can withstand light winds, the tall plumes can be damaged by very strong gusts. Think about how exposed you are to the wind in your intended spot, and take precautions as needed.

• Pick a spot that's convenient for tending to the garden, such cutting back overgrown branches or pulling out diseased plants. Exercise caution when planting near walkways or other place where someone could accidentally brush up against the leaves' pointed tips.

- Think about how pampas grass will look in your garden. Its texture and intrigue it brings to the garden make it a popular choice for both focal points and background plants.

- Think about the weather patterns in your area. Even though pampas grass can tolerate a lot of various weather, it could look different when you plant it in places where the weather is really hot or cold.

You may choose a spot for growing pampas grass that is both healthy for it and beautiful for your garden or landscape if you give careful thought to these things. For information that is specific to your area, it's best to consult gardening professionals or extension agencies in your area.

Establishing Pampas Grass

For pampas grass to establish itself and grow healthily, there are a number of things that need to be done while planting the grass. In general, when planting pampas grass, follow these steps:

• After the soil has warmed and the danger of frost has gone, the best time to sow pampas grass is in the late spring or early summer. This gives the plant time to set down roots before winter sets in.

• The soil must be able to drain effectively. To enhance drainage, amend clay or heavy soils with organic materials like compost.

• Take a reading of the soil's pH; a neutral to slightly acidic soil (between 6.0 and 7.0) is ideal for Pampas grass.

• Pampas grass requires at least six to eight hours of direct sunlight per day, so be sure to pick a spot that gets enough of sunshine. Avoid overcrowding and give plants plenty of room to grow before they reach maturity.

• At a depth equal to and wider than the pampas grass plant's root ball, dig a hole. This will give the roots ample space to grow. Space pampas grass plants according to their variety's mature width if you're planting more than one.

• With caution, remove the pampas grass from its container, taking care not to damage it with the sharp leaves. Fill in the space around the plant with a combination of the current soil and organic debris after placing it in the middle of the hole. To help the dirt settle around the plant's roots, water it deeply.

• If you want your newly seeded pampas grass to take root, you need to water it frequently in the first several weeks. After it has taken root, pampas grass can withstand periods of drought rather well. For optimal moisture retention, weed suppression, and soil temperature regulation, mulch the area surrounding the plant's base.

• Trim pampas grass just before new growth appears, either in the late winter or early spring. To avoid cuts from the leaves' sharp edges, wear gloves. Shape the plant to your liking by cutting back unhealthy or diseased leaves. Remove just the necessary amount of green growth; too much can stunt blossoming.

• Look for symptoms of pests or diseases on a regular basis; respond accordingly. If the plant gets too big or congested, divide it every few years. Keep an eye on its growth.

Keep in mind that pampas grass can be invasive in some areas, so it's important to research and follow any rules that may be in place. If you follow these instructions to the letter, you should have no trouble planting and caring for pampas grass in your yard.

CHAPTER FOUR
Pasture Maintenance

Watering, trimming, and general upkeep are the three basic components of pampas grass care. Pampas grass need special attention, therefore here is how to do it:

• During the first several weeks following planting, water the pampas grass often to aid in the establishment of a robust root system. Make sure the soil is always damp, but not soggy. Once established, pampas grass can withstand moderate levels of drought. Overwatering can cause root rot, so it's important to water deeply during lengthy dry spells but let the soil dry out in between.

- Before new growth starts, in late winter or early spring, prune pampas grass. To protect yourself from the sharp edges of the leaves, wear gloves and other protective gear.

- Defoliating: Trim away any diseased or otherwise unhealthy leaves that are close to the plant's base. This encourages the creation of new, healthy tissue.

- Shaping: To keep the plant looking neat and appealing, trim its outside edges. If you want your plants to bloom, you shouldn't hack into their greenery too much.

- Pampas grass doesn't need much food, but a balanced, slow-release fertilizer applied in the spring will help it grow strong and healthy. Overfertilization can cause foliage to become excessively lush, thus it's best to avoid it.

• Put some mulch around the plant's base to keep the soil moist, prevent weeds, and control the soil's temperature. To avoid problems caused by excess moisture, keep mulch at least a few inches away from the plant's crown.

• Be vigilant about the aggressive spread of pampas grass in the region. To avoid damaging local ecosystems, it is crucial to control the plant, as some types are invasive.

- If you want to keep your pampas grass plants healthy and avoid overpopulation, you should divide big clumps every few years. Doing this in the late winter or early spring is the norm.

- To prevent the accumulation of snow and ice, which can cause the plumes to break, it is recommended to tie the plumes together in areas with severe winter weather.

- Keep an eye out for pests like aphids and scale insects on the plant and remove them as necessary. Be vigilant in your search for diseases, such rust or fungal infections, and act swiftly to address any that you find.

To ensure the long-term health and beauty of your pampas grass, it is important to regularly evaluate its status and respond quickly to any changes. Consider the local climate and the plant's unique traits while making adjustments to its care routine.

Landscape Architecture With Grass Of The Pampas

Because of its height, texture, and dramatic potential, pampas grass is a great plant to incorporate into landscape design. Some ways to use pampas grass in landscaping are as follows:

• Place a cluster of pampas grass plants in a prominent spot in your yard or landscaping. The towering plumes have the potential to become a show-stopping focal point.

• Make use of pampas grass to create an organic windbreak or privacy screen. It adds visual appeal and a feeling of enclosure when planted in a row along a property line or surrounding an outdoor seating area.

• To set the stage for other garden elements, scatter pampas grass around. It may amplify the sense of depth and dimension in a design with its towering stature and delicate plumes.

- Plant pampas grass with other beautiful grasses, shrubs, and perennials in a mixed-flower garden. A varied and ever-changing scenery is the result of this.

- Pampas grass can be grown in ornamental pots or huge containers. For smaller spaces or to make patios and balconies seem taller, this is a great choice.

- Pampas grass complements native grasses and plants in gardens that aim for a more rustic or natural look. It can evoke a sensation of motion and evoke images of tall grasses found in nature.

- Pampas grass thrives in areas with water features, including fountains or ponds. The water's reflection in the ethereal plumes can be a striking visual contrast.

- Pampas grass is a year-round landscape focal point. While the plumes put on a spectacular show in the late summer and early fall, the grass keeps its beauty even in the dead of winter.

- To help control erosion, plant pampas grass on hills. The vast root system has the potential to stabilize soil and reduce the likelihood of runoff.

- Pampas grass is a great way to give your landscape a visual and textural contrast. Combine it with plants that display a variety of leaf shapes and hues to create an eye-catching arrangement.

Additionally, choose non-invasive kinds of pampas grass or adhere to local rules to avoid the undesirable spread of this plant, which can be invasive in some areas.

CHAPTER FIVE
Time Of Year Factors

When caring for and incorporating pampas grass into your landscape, it's vital to consider the changes that occur throughout the year. Take the following into account based on the season:

1. Seasonal Change:

• The best time to prune pampas grass is in the late winter or early spring, when you can easily remove any damaged or dead leaves. This keeps it in a presentable form while also encouraging new growth.

• Fertilization: If appropriate, use a balanced, slow-release fertilizer over the soil in the early spring to supply nutrients for the crop.

2. Season: Summer

• Even while pampas grass can withstand dry spells once it's established, it could need a little more watering in the summer.

• When does Pampas grass usually bloom? Usually between the end of summer and the beginning of October. Take pleasure in the airy plumes that adorn your yard.

3. Season changes:

• The fall landscape is adorned with the enduring plumes of pampas grass, a sign that the blooming process is far from over.

• Seed Heads: If you aren't worried about the plant self-seeding, you can give it a decorative boost by leaving the seed heads on display all winter long.

4. In the winter:

• Slumber: During the winter months, Pampas grass enters a dormant state and its leaves could become brown. This happens all the time during a plant's life cycle.

• The best time to clip pampas grass before new growth starts is in late January, during winter pruning.

Handle the leaves with care, since they might be sharp.

5. Every Day:

• Maintain vigilance in the region to make sure pampas grass isn't aggressively expanding and taking over. If necessary, take the necessary steps to manage its expansion.

• Keep an eye out for pests and illnesses by checking the plant on a regular basis; deal with any problems as soon as you see them.

6. Severe Weather:

• Enduring the Winter: If you live in a region that gets a lot of snow and ice, you might want to think about tying the plumes together so they don't break.

• Support the tall plumes of pampas grass so they don't get damaged by strong winds if you live in an area that gets them.

7. Seasonal Preparation:

• Planning for Seasonal Interest: Think about how pampas grass will look at different times of year while you're planning your landscaping. Fall and winter are prime times to see its towering stature and dazzling plumes.

Your pampas grass will be healthy, beautiful, and blended into your environment all year round if you keep these seasonal factors in mind. The unique requirements of each season, as well as the regional climate, should inform your adjustments to the plant's care routine.

Methods For Propagation

The most popular ways to propagate pampas grass are by division and seed, although cuttings are a less common option. A tutorial on these propagation methods is provided here:

1. Division:

• Optimal Timing: Before new growth starts, in late winter or early spring, is when pampas grass is best divided.

Action:

- Removing the mature pampas grass cluster requires digging.

- Cut the clump into tiny pieces using a sharp spade or a saw. Incorporate a section of the root system and multiple healthy shoots into each division.

- Make sure to water the divisions thoroughly and replant them at the same depth as before.

Seeds for harvesting:

- Gather seeds in the fall from fully developed seed heads.

- Shake or comb the seed heads after they have dried on the plant to extract the seeds.

Plant seeds:

- Place the seeds approximately 1/4 inch deep in a seed-starting mix and sow them in the late winter or early spring.

- Up until the seeds sprout, make sure the soil is always damp.

- Transfer seedlings to individual pots or the garden as soon as they reach a suitable size.

2. Cuts (Lower Frequency):

• Root cuttings are a less popular way to cultivate Pampas grass, while basal offshoots are another option.

Action:

• Pick a mature plant that is in good health and has deep roots.

• Partially slice the root or a shoot that has roots attached using a sterile knife that is sharp.

• The cutting can be planted either in a container filled with soil that drains well or straight into the garden. Until the cutting grows roots, the soil should be kept continually damp.

Guidelines for Fruitful Propagation:

- Select only healthy plants from which to harvest seeds, cuttings, or divisions.

- To avoid problems like root rot, plant on soil that drains effectively.

- During the establishment phase, make sure to provide enough moisture.

- The distinctive big plumes of pampas grass may not appear for a while, so be patient.

- Keep in mind that pampas grass has the potential to become an invasive species in certain areas. It is important to research local rules and laws before planting or propagating this plant so it does not become a problem in natural settings.

Pick a way of propagation that works for you and your environment the best; next, modify your strategy according to the traits of the pampas grass type you're dealing with.

CHAPTER SIX
Troubleshooting And Common Problems

Even while pampas grass is usually rather tough, it still has its share of problems. Some typical issues with pampas grass and ways to fix them are as follows:

1. Too Much Water:

• Root rot, leaf yellowing or withering, and other symptoms.

• A solution would be to use soil that drains well and to let it dry out in between waterings. If needed, water less frequently.

2. Low water level:

• Markers: Growth retardation, browning of the leaf tips, and dryness.

• When the weather becomes dry, water the plant thoroughly. Until it becomes established, newly planted pampas grass could need additional watering.

3. Subpar Drainage of Soil:

• Root rot, leaf yellowing, and overall decrease are symptoms.

• To fix this, add organic material to heavy or clay soils so they drain better. Prevent standing water.

4. Spreading Adversely:

- A sign of Pampas grass is its aggressive proliferation outside of its allotted area.

- If possible, select non-invasive variants. Keep an eye on the plant and divide it or otherwise manage its spread on a regular basis. Find out what the rules are in your area about how invasive it could be.

5. The Fungal Illnesses:

- Lesions, staining, or discoloration on leaves can be signs of rust or another fungal illness.

- To fix this, you should make sure air is flowing freely, not water from above, and think about using fungicides if the issue continues. Take down any diseased plants and throw them away.

6. Unwanted Entities:

• Pampas grass can be infested by aphids, scale insects, or mites.

• To get rid of bugs, use neem oil or insecticidal soap. Remove severely contaminated sections and dispose of them.

7. Winter Debris:

• Browning of leaves as a result of cold stress or injury is one symptom.

- A simple way to prevent snow and ice from accumulating on the plumes is to tie them together before winter. Pampas grass thrives in somewhat shaded areas.

8. Tip Browning on Leaves:

- The tips of the leaves may become dry or brown, which is a common symptom, particularly in hot and dry weather.

- Solution: Make sure the plant has enough water, particularly when the weather gets hot. Remove any tips that are discolored or dead.

9. Pruning Errors:

• Warning Signs: If you prune your plants too severely, they may not be able to produce flowers or stay healthy in general.

• Solution: Cut back on the healthy, green parts of the plant as little as possible, and only remove diseased or otherwise unhealthy leaves.

10. The Discordance of Soil pH:

• Yellowing leaves and stunted development are symptoms.

• Approach: Check the soil's pH level and add lime or other amendments as needed to keep it at a slightly acidic to neutral range (around 6.0 to 7.0).

You can help your pampas grass stay healthy and vibrant by keeping an eye out for symptoms of stress, pests, or diseases and taking care of them as soon as you notice them. Care for your pampas grass as directed by the variety you have and the weather where you live.

Grass Harvesting On The Pampas

The main reason to harvest pampas grass is for its decorative plumes, which may be used in crafts and indoor arrangements. The following is a manual for collecting pampas grass:

• When the plumes of pampas grass are fully mature and have acquired their distinctive fluffy look, which is in late summer to fall, it is the best time to harvest the grass.

• Select plumes that have reached full maturity; they will have feathery seed heads that are delicate and fluffy.

• Do Not Harvest Plumes That Are Not entirely Mature: Plumes that are not entirely mature should not be harvested since they may not have reached the size and texture that is desired.

• Clean, Sharp Shears or Pruners: For a precise cut, use clean, sharp shears or pruners.

• Hand Protection: To avoid cuts from the leaves, dress in long sleeves and gloves.

• Begin at the Base: Place your shears or pruners near the base of the plume, close to where it branches out from the main plant, and cut there.

• The length and appearance of the plume can be preserved by making a clean, diagonal cut.

- Remember to leave a sufficient amount of foliage on the plant when harvesting in order to keep it healthy in general. Because they contribute to the plant's ability to generate energy, the green leaves should not be chopped too severely.

- After harvesting, hang the plumes upside down in a dry, well-ventilated place after tying them together in little bundles.

- Drying Period: Make sure the plumes dry entirely. Depending on the relative humidity and air circulation, this can take a few weeks.

- For interior arrangements, dried plumes of pampas grass are a popular choice. Make them a part of a dried flower arrangement or put them in a vase. Pampas grass is versatile and may be utilized in a variety of crafts, including wreaths, dried flower crowns, and home decor projects.

• Keep the plumes away from mold and mildew by storing them in a dry location after they have dried completely.

• Look for Seeds: Keep in mind that seeds can spread invasive plants, so be careful while dealing with them. Before taking the plumes home, shake or comb them over a container to gather any loose seeds.

- When harvesting, it's a good idea to leave a few plumes on the plant so it can naturally reseed and regenerate.

If pampas grass is deemed an invasive species in your area, it is extremely important to adhere to local restrictions and procedures when harvesting it. To keep plants healthy and stop seeds from getting into the wrong places, it's important to harvest them in a responsible way.

CHAPTER SEVEN
Considerations And Impact On The Environment

Depending on the situation, the area, and the particular traits of the plant, pampas grass (Cortaderia spp.) can have either beneficial or bad effects on the ecosystem. Important factors to consider while dealing with pampas grass in terms of the environment are:

Environmental Benefits:

• Because of its deep root structure, pampas grass is useful for preventing soil erosion on hillsides and slopes. Soil stabilization and runoff prevention are both aided by the roots.

• Little animals, like insects and birds, can find a home in the thick mats of pampas grass.

- Responsibly utilizing pampas grass enhances biodiversity while creating visually appealing gardens and landscapes.

Disadvantages to the Environment:

- In certain areas, especially those with a Mediterranean climate, pampas grass is seen as an invasive plant. It has the potential to reduce biodiversity by outcompeting local vegetation.

- The wind is a powerful vector for the rapid dissemination of pampas grass seeds. Because of this, it has the ability to invade new places through seed dispersal.

- The invasive pampas grass has the potential to change the dynamics of ecosystems and displace native species, both of which have detrimental effects on native plant groups.

- In areas where wildfires are common, the parched leaves of pampas grass can be a serious fire risk. The extremely combustible quality of the plant makes it a potential fire starter.

- Although pampas grass can withstand periods of drought once it has taken root, it may need a substantial amount of water while it is just getting started. This can pose a problem in areas where water is scarce.

Growing and Managing in an Eco-Friendly Manner:

• Choose non-invasive varieties of pampas grass when landscaping to reduce the risk of unintended spread.

• Make sure you know the rules in your area about growing pampas grass. Restrictions or guidelines may be in place in certain areas to stop its spread.

• To avoid the spread of seeds, prune responsibly. If you are worried about pampas grass spreading, remove the seed heads before they mature.

- It is important to follow local guidelines when using herbicides or conducting regular monitoring if pampas grass becomes an invasive plant in a specific area.

- Inform the locals of the possible effects of pampas grass on the environment. Get the word out about how to manage your garden responsibly.

In conclusion, pampas grass does have some positive effects on the environment, but its invasiveness and the damage it could do to native ecosystems need serious thought and responsible management. It's vital to know the plant's traits, local rules, and the possible effects of growing it in various ecological settings.

Summary

Pampas grass, scientifically known as Cortaderia spp., is an adaptable and aesthetically pleasing plant that, when cared for properly, can enrich landscapes. Nevertheless, in areas where it is known to be invasive, it is particularly important to thoroughly assess the environmental impact and related considerations. Important considerations are as follows:

• Aesthetic Value: Pampas grass is a popular decorative grass because it adds height, visual interest, and texture to landscapes.

• Soil Stabilization and Slope Erosion Control: The plant's extensive root system can help stabilize soil and reduce slope erosion.

Difficult Points:

• Invasiveness: In certain areas, pampas grass is seen as an invasive plant that threatens local ecosystems by replacing native plants.

• The invasive potential of pampas grass is heightened by its high seed production and its easy dispersal.

• Dry vegetation, particularly in regions vulnerable to wildfires, can create a fire hazard.

Ethical Leadership:

• Minimize the Risk of Unintentional Spread by Selecting Non-Invasive Varieties(PIVs).

• Make Sure You Know and Follow Any Requirements for Growing Pampas Grass in Your Area.

• Minimize Seed Production and Spread by Pruning With Care: Minimize seed production and plant spread by pruning with care.

• Education for the Environment: Get the word out about the possible effects of pampas grass cultivation on the environment and encourage responsible methods of cultivation.

It is crucial for environmentally conscious landscaping to strike a balance between the pampas grass's visual appeal and its possible ecological impact.

One way to enjoy pampas grass without negatively impacting the environment is to choose non-invasive varieties, follow local guidelines, and encourage responsible cultivation and management practices. Proper care for ornamental plants, such as pampas grass, requires both environmental consciousness and environmental education.

THE END

www.ingramcontent.com/pod-product-compliance
Lightning Source LLC
LaVergne TN
LVHW021648200325
806457LV00008B/493